THE RATIONAL APPROACH TO CHOOSE YOUR CAREER

EXPLORE YOUR POWER OF THINKING AND CHOOSE YOUR DESTINY.

MOHAMMED MUSTAFA ALI

CONTENTS

Title Page 1

Introduction 5

Preface 7

Chapter I 9

Chapter II 15

Chapter III 22

Chapter IV 29

Chapter V 34

Chapter VI 38

Chapter VII 43

Chapter VIII 47

Chapter IX 52

Chapter X 57

Chapter XI 59

About The Author 63

INTRODUCTION

As an author of this book, I would like to share some insightful information which I believe is more important in career choices we made during our high school, Intermediate, Bachelor's and Master's degree. Education is one of the most important aspects of modern society. The things which influence our choices are mostly our friends, family, relatives, money etc., the most important one is what do you have in your mind when you decide or take a choice subconsciously and consciously. Moreover, how far you can imagine about yourself in that role, how close is your imagination with the practicality of that role. Your happiness and interest should be the basis of the decision. My audience is every reader but majorly the students who are at teenage and the parents who wants their kids to be successful in life with their own choices and if they failed also as the reality is harsh it will be by their own decisions after understanding the scenario of life and be courageous to accept their mistakes and start over. With this book at last you will accomplish facts of decision making by considering your own choice, learning about imagination of your career and measuring with practicality, avoiding the influence and pressure of the society and avoiding the rat race. So, let's get started...

PREFACE

I am thankful to Allah for everything and to everyone who I know and to whom I even met once in my life. So, one way or the other everyone has taught me to become what I am today but, majorly my family has supported me a lot without them and by the grace of Allah I wouldn't be an author.

CHAPTER I

Evaluation of Grades

Grades

Grades in one way represent individual capabilities in each subject you just have to identify in which subjects you are getting good grades consistently and if you could identify the reason behind that will be an advantage. Suppose you are getting good grades in math as per that you can explore your options which majorly involves math in your career.

Possibility as per the grades

Once you had analyzed and identify the subjects in which you are getting good grades then you can list out all the possible options which involves those subjects as major contribution in that profession respectively.

Interest and grade

Identifying your interest of profession and choosing carefully among your career options is the easiest and toughest part depending on the individual interest and grades, some of them might be good in grades but their interest lies in some physical profession like an athlete or a boxer in this case your grades will not be the basis of selection of your profession but your physical strength will play an important role in determining the profession.

If someone decided a career as a boxer or an athlete or an actor or anything which is not so common will differentiate them from following the rat race. Family support is important at this stage but for these professions your family might oppose your move which eventually make you will feel a little depressed and pressurized if they want you to take some common option of their choice like engineer or doctor which is okay to pursue if your interest permits in the end your interest and your passion for something will help you attain success later in life, if you had chosen something which you are not interested by following rat race or by the pressure of your parents you will end up regretting things later in life. Every day you will have to work make a living by that profession which you don't like, you wouldn't be happy in the morning to even wake up and you don't want to be the one.

So, it is important for you to follow your passion at the very early stage of life and if your family oppose you have to make them realize with patience that you want to pursue and follow your passion. If you choose something which you are not interested you will end up doing that throughout your life and you wouldn't be happy about it.

<u>Niche career</u>

Exploring niche career options before taking a decision about your career is very important as in the early stage of life you will not be familiar with lot of professions you must have heard about the ones which are famous and popular or the ones you came across within your family and friend's circle. So, it's important that as per your grades you have to find way to explore all the possibilities as this will be your homework which be worth throughout your life.

<u>Explore your career</u>

Professional exploration of chosen career is indeed important as it plays a very important criteria in deciding your career or say finalizing it. The depth of understanding and exploring of your selected career will depend on the knowledge you possess at the time of choosing your career options. After choosing the career option in early stage (i.e., at 11th & Bachelor's) there are still further options need to be chosen as you grow you will get close to the last option when you decided to specialize by pursuing MSc or PHD.

Consider my example in my case I decided to become a petroleum engineer but I was not aware with the familiarity of the working environment I will be faced after completion of my degree. Petroleum engineer will be exposed to dangerous gases with smell like rotten eggs which I couldn't bare in a refinery or at a well head from where the crude oil gets extracted and the risk factor associated is also high not every company will follow the complete safety measures in reality. Well destiny made me quit that job but I was still in the oil field but working inside the office.

The point of sharing my story is to elaborate and explore your selected career option deeply to get clarity as how you will end up working in that profession and whether you will like the working environment or not. If you had a chance at early stage of choosing your career to know about the working environment or if by chance you have selected something similar in which your family and friends are working take their opinion about the working environment so you will have a rough idea or if possible ask someone you know in a good position or own that business to visit with them and see it for a day how is the working environment and remember it might not be the same for you till the time you start your career but before choosing that career you will have a basic reality experience and idea of how you will start your journey after your completion of degree.

<u>Avoiding complexity</u>

Avoiding complexion of anything is a very great skill which can be mastered with time, majority of the time our minds will lose focus from the solution and get involved in the problem making it more problematic, the first thing in order to avoid complexity is to avoid doing this mistake always make sure your working approach is towards the solution this will be the rule number 1 to avoid complexity.

While avoiding complexity for some people it could be hard because they have a lot in mind which doesn't relate with the problem, they should keep that aside to solve it with a clear mind and understanding the clarity of the problem is very important in solving anything in life, if required it should be broken down in steps and if there are multiple solutions for the problem after careful consideration of the options we should proceed with the most suitable solution.

In some cases, you have to write down all the options and check individually the most suitable one, for example if someone got stuck in two different options with their grades and interest both simultaneously then you have to perform deep analysis of both the options separately and identify the basis of interest in both the career options. For example, if someone wants to choose to be a mechanical engineer because he like cars and want to work in automotive industry in future to build cars as a professional but just on the basis of someone liking it will not be enough to proceed with that option, we should perform some deep analysis as why do you like cars, if his interest is to just ride it or own it, then he may or not like to work on engines. So, in order to avoid complexity, the clarity of the problem and its depth should be understood which will eventually make decisions easy and suitable.

Amount of hard work to get good grades

Hard work is very important in life but there is difference between ability to do hard work and struggle to do hard work. Some subjects are easy and hard depending on the individual, some students find something hard but for other students that will be easy based on their hard work, intellect and understanding of the subject. Degree of hard and easy varies with each subject and student. While choosing your career you must consider the hard work you put in to get good grades in different subjects this hard work which I am discussing is not one time hard work that you have faced due to some uncertain situation in family or friends or your illness during exams but the consistency of hard work you put in throughout your academics or over the years. This will help you take a clear decision about your career option.

Easily getting good grades with disinterest in the subject

Good grades are always result of hard work but, sometimes if we are good at a certain subject we find it easy to get good grades in other subject but, strange we don't find that subject to be interested this might happen in such cases we have to identify our strength of getting good grades and the basis of why we are not interested in that subject. Suppose if someone is good at math's he will be good in other subjects where math is required as part of the subject and might be because of this they are getting good grades irrespective of their own interest in that subject.

The basis of our strength is very important in selection of career choice and that basis should be the major base of your career choice. Suppose if someone is getting good grades in physics because his calculation skills are good and that individual decided to proceed further taking physics as the base but, his chosen career does not majorly involved his actual strength will end up making an incorrect choice without being aware of it. Careful analysis of your strength and basis in the subjects are very important factor which leads to decide the best suitable career choice.

Failure in grades despite of interest in the Subject

Failure is part of the life not the end of it and it is the beginning of the success for the people who doesn't quit and avoid the mistakes of the past in their next attempt. some individual unfortunately will end up having bad grades despite their interest in the subject very rarely it happen due to some personal reason or illness they couldn't able to perform this shouldn't be the reason to avoid that subject from one of your career options this might happen not once but twice or even thrice that you consistently not performing in that subject you have to identify the reason why you are lacking behind in that subject sometimes, you will be interested in some part of the subject which doesn't constitute major part of the questionnaire in the exam. so, you might end up getting not so good grades in that subject despite of your interest in part of that subject. You can still proceed to consider this as the career option if you are really interested and your future career option which you are deciding should be majorly based on the part of the subject which you are interested in, to make things clear a thorough very well deep insight knowledge of the career option which you are selecting is very important in this case.

Grades evaluation by Teacher hard/easy

Evaluation of grades are important and evaluator as well, in some cases it might happen that the evaluator is easy in providing good grades for all the students and not many students failed in that subject, the evaluator will be kind hearted in providing grades and sometimes the evaluator will teach you the same subject over the years so, your results when you analyze will be good for all those years. So in such cases we have to be honest to our self and consider the evaluator kindness in providing grades in our selection of our career through grades it does look like a minor thing in some cases but, in some cases if this is the subject that a candidate will be proceeding forward then it might impact his decision for the career depending on the genuinely of the evaluation.

Conclusion

At last from this chapter we have covered almost all the important criteria to consider in order to choose career options based on the grades or physical fitness or whatever skills are required depending on the individual case.

CHAPTER II

Finding Your Interest

Discover your Interests

Discovering your interests, finding your passion is easy and hard depending on the nature of the individual but it's worth every dime putting your efforts to discover your interest as this will or could be the thing you will be deciding to do throughout your life without getting bored or frustrated or waiting for vacation as majority of the people in today's world are doing and will continue to do so if things wouldn't change and the change is not from the outside but from the inside that is the individual personality and its thinking has to be changed as to not to follow the rat race to get away from this problem.

In one way I find the thinking of doing anything is very important but that will not accomplish anything until you put efforts and act on it and this is the real basis of the problem which I did described above people tends to think they will change their career as majority of them are not happy that is the reason they want to change but, many few will actually change it rest of them which is majority will just think about it or mostly talk about doing so. The reason I have illustrated the present scenario as to make you realize how important it is to discover your interests at the early stage of life and having a sense of understanding and getting more informative on the subjects you like about it will make it easier for you to discover your passion for something. In order to start discovering your passion list out all the things which you like irrespective of its nature of work or play but make sure you only list out those things which you like doing the rest of your life and will not get tired of doing every day for some individuals the list will include a lot of options and for some few don't worry about the numbers if you have few you must have chosen it carefully.

Basis of Selection of Interest

Once you have discovered the list of works you are interested to proceed as career options in your life you got to identify what are the basis of selection of those options you mentioned in the list it might differ or same for some options, having a sense to identify the basis of interest at early stage of life might be difficult or easy depending on the individual if you couldn't identify that's okay but, if you could identify the basis of interest and look through it individually with each option you will be exploring the basis of interest of your options.

Suppose if someone likes cricket as an option as in India majority of them like to play cricket and want to choose a career in it but intention will differ with every individual as per their own interest of basis as someone likes to bat he enjoyed batting and playing cricket but for some individual the basis will be fame not the game, fame definitely comes when your pure interests of basis is the game of cricket but it might be difficult if your base is fame or something else. So it's very important to identify the basis of interest if one can do it's worth your life and to able to understand the base is the game not the fame will make you successful.

Influencing Criteria Determine

There are lot of things in life that can be influential or inspiring for you to attain something or to be successful in life but, sometimes we unknowingly or subconsciously take decisions without consideration of influential criteria behind the basis of our interest in that decision which is normal as majority of the people tends to do but, if you could identify the influencing criteria behind your major decisions of life it will be easier for you specially, if you have to choose from many options as in our case as a career choice we will have multiple options listed out and exploring it with the basis of interest is the first level of thinking and the next level will be to determine the influencing criteria behind that very base of interest.

The purpose should be your selection of options and your choice from that be clear of complexion, if you consider the same case of cricket the base of someone interest to select career in cricket is batting then the influencing criteria as what makes that individual select batting as his interest needs to be identified, that's gives you deep level of understanding about your own options which will after careful prioritization among your options will be the one career choice for your life.

Distinguish between Interest and Wish

An individual has to understand the difference consciously throughout his life or at least during the time of active thinking between interest and wish. An interest is something which you can't live without it or if you can't have it you won't stop trying to achieve it but, a wish is something you can live without it and you may or not be putting efforts to achieve it or you will be just simply waiting for the thing to be happen to complete your wish. When you do take a career choice make sure you are following the path of interest not a wish which will be a waste of time until you realize the wish will not come true unless you take action on it.

Exploring the path to reach Interest

Successfully exploring the path to reach your goal in which you got your interest plays a very important role to identify the intermediate steps and setting up smaller goals on the path which will finally lead to your ultimate career choice. You got to be very careful about the possible setbacks in the path or identifying multiple options on the path it will be better for you to know about the smaller options to choose during the path exploration which might majorly effect on your ultimate career choice. Advancement of your path is inevitable as you will be growing with experience, your path or plan will be updated accordingly with the utmost reality you can experience at that point of time. So, always find the ways to update the path in more real form to attain your goal in a smooth manner.

Identification of Hardships

Hardships are part of any journey you take in life but to identify it's presence without neglecting it will help your journey to be of less hassle. While most of the times, we can identify the forthcoming hardship sometimes, we tend to neglect it by our own overconfidence that it will not impact you, the level of requirement of thinking of an individual matters a lot in order to be prepared on the solution for the hardships.

Sometimes, we come across unidentified hardships these are the ones for which you have to be conscious about all the time, it's not only the hardships which you have identified in your journey there are more to come in your way as you grow with your experience you will keep adding it to your routine of work in your journey. Sometimes our neglection towards working to resolve a problem in our journey or our laziness will cost us dearly and some hardships are so interconnected with series of events that will leave a major impact on your journey or even break you at a point of time so, always be focused to avoid this situation.

Mental Readiness and Acceptance of Hardships

In all of the things in the world a person wouldn't be defeated by anyone but from itself before he get defeated by the opponent or in any circumstances in life he will get defeated mentally first, the mental readiness plays important role in life as you grow your mental powers should grow and become more stronger as you go through hardships in your journey. So, always be prepared mentally and physically for the tasks of your routine and accept the hardships coming across during the routine by identifying them without neglecting it. The hardships once identified will give time for you to prepare to overcome it with your practice and it will not be considered as hardship anymore as it will become easy for you as you work on it.

Taking Interest as Priority over Hardships

In life you will come across a lot of situations, where you are stuck in with the choices you have to choose to proceed in life as you grow your decision making skills or the choices you choose should grow because you are in the end a product of your own choices. So, it's very important to work on decision making skills. Being said that always look through your interest carefully just because of something that is part of your interest in career is associated with a hardship don't give up that choice in your career.

Let me illustrate that with an example of cricket if someone chooses that to be his career option as some of them only like to bat and doesn't like to field or find it hard to field they are not as good as when they bat. So, if you are really interested in cricket to bat you should choose that as your career option, always choose interest as priority over hardships which can overcome with time by practice.

Breaking down the Steps of Work Routine

Breaking down the steps of your work plays important role in selection of your interest, once you have listed out the options for your career then breakdown of each option in detail as much as you can with the help of someone in that field or online by any source this basically implies a full typical day of your chosen career that you will be aware of all the possible major or minor things you will have to go through and you can measure the worthiness of your interest and priority. In this way it will be easy for you to choose your career option and indirectly you will be aware of the work routine and will be mentally ready for the work as you wouldn't be surprise or shock with the things when actually you have to perform when time comes.

Priorities of your Life and Financial Aid in your Life

Understanding the priorities of your life along with the current and possible future responsibilities and by keeping in mind your financial stability of your family are very important things to consider during the decision making of your career. There are very few people at young age understand their own and possible future responsibilities and their dependency financially on their parents until they start earning and at which stage the family finances stands until they begin to earn whether, the earning person of the family head will be retired before you will start earning or anything. You have to be very careful to consider this criteria while choosing the career but, that doesn't mean one should give up on their interest, you always have to find a way to do things which you like and when it comes to the choice of your career that will be filled with major part of your life so, you have be very careful while you choose your career.

Finalization of Interest as per Priority

After careful selection of your listed options for your career you have to prioritize your list according to your level of interest in each option. You can do this as you have broken down the steps for each work option based on the internal steps and interest towards each internal work option or based on your level of interest. Moreover, considering your financial ability, hardships and all the aspects you can finalize your interested career option among the multiple options which you have listed.

CHAPTER III

Imagination Of Routine

Future Mindset

The selection of your career options through imagining it's routine that you will go through in a long run of your career time and everyday routine at different levels of your career gives your career decision a practical edge for future mindsets of the things you come across in your career journey.

Imagination of your Work Routine

Everyone, when it comes to career choice will have some imagination in their mind which is relatable to sometimes close enough or will be completely different from its practical world. You got to learn to imagine things in detail and more closure to the practicality in order to avoid disappointment which will be caused through your own deviation of imagination from the reality.

Routine of Selected Work

The routine of selected work of your career option can be discovered at different levels of your career from the present point when you imagine or discover the routine people tends to look through major things at different career levels of the selected option by ignoring the detail of the routine which they will face on everyday basis. you got to make sure you have lived your life hypothetically in your imagination with all the possible aspects you can cover in your imagination in order to have a clear picture of the choice you have chosen for your career.

Comparing your Imagination with Practicality (Statistics)

When we imagine a lot we tend to forget that is imagination and feel the imagination to be the reality which may or may not be true depends on how close your imagination is to the reality and how much it actually deviates from it. In order to perform the reality check you have to check the statistics of the choice of your career option and moreover, whatever you can get to perform the comparison between imagination and reality just take and do it. It's not the actuality that we want but, how imaginative are we from the real world of our career choice.

At different levels of timeline of your career you might have to upgrade, just check the facts how many people of the same caliber are at the progressive or promotional level of your imagination with your imaginative timeline or how much deviated are you from your imagination. This will help you a lot to get you on track if deviated.

True to Yourself

Always be true to yourself , the biggest cheat a man can do is to cheat himself by not being true to himself which will harm your future if not corrected at the right time. There are many ways in life which a person consciously or subconsciously will not be true to him as he will be afraid to face the truth as always the reality will be harsh to digest. but, it is always be easier to face it in the beginning rather than late as it's get worse with the time. Always remember to take the honest road Specially, when it's all about your life.

Setting Higher Limits and Overestimate Yourself

The nature of human being varies individually with different personalities, we tend to be biased in our favor when it comes to our present and future outcomes. Some people overestimate themself when setting some career goals or limits this could happen when we overlook our actions, our lack of implementation in practice that will deviate us being the person who estimated at the beginning which at later stage becomes overestimated as our required actions are not in the manner to achieve those higher limits which we set up in our long time career plan.

It's not that you cannot achieve the higher limits which has been set up it's just that you are more courageous when it comes to planning the limits but not when it's comes to implementation of required action to attain that higher limits nothing is impossible with the right determination, focus and consistency anything can be achieved you just got to know your present value, your present caliber and the higher limits which you are setting up for yourself you got to identify what it will take for you to develop within yourself in order to attain those higher limits and implement it every single day.

Setting Lower Limits and Underestimate Yourself

As mentioned above nature of human beings varies, by setting up lower limits and underestimating yourself will be harmful in many ways as the person might not think of himself good enough to raise the limits higher, this could be because of the past disappointment that in past someone might have not up to the mark as planned and missed their own limits set by them this in turn could put off the person to lower the limits and to be settle for lower than of which someone is capable off. The circumstances and situation will varies widely with the time and one should consider this while putting any limits along with it. If someone is hardworking he got to think that he is working smart enough to reach those limits or not just being depressed about the past and setting the limits lower. The limits can be anything related to your career or personal goals but it got to bring a smile on your face that's all it matters. There is no comparison of goals with anyone when it comes to happiness, as its criteria varies with every individual you better find your real happy goals to hit.

Encountering Hardships in the Routine

Every individual in life at some point or daily will encounter hardships in one or other way and it varies with person to person a hardship for someone will be not be a hardship for the other, same applies to things which you find it easy might be hard for someone else it's just how well you know the things, how much correct information you got about anything you considered as hardship. I would like to emphasize again I did mention the word "correct" information that is more important when receiving the information about getting through your hardships. Identifying before which hardships could be encountered on calculative basis, will make a person to be prepared mentally and physically to go through it as he will be aware of it, if he is prepared well enough the hardships will no longer be hard. In this process of identifying hardships and working on its solution an individual will develop their personality and built-in confidence, as the possibilities of the hardships which he will come across in his routine will be known to him.

Working for You or for Someone Else

The nature of people working is majorly categorized in two ways either you are working for yourself or someone else, anything you choose among the options that is completely up to you and it's your right but, being conscious of to whom you work is very important if you are an employee then you are working for someone else it indirectly you are fulfilling someone else dreams and getting paid for it, if you choose to be an entrepreneur in your choice of your career then you are working for yourself directly as in the former option you will be working for yourself with your own choice but the growth rate will not be the same when compared with latter and moreover, you got to identify or prepare yourself in which category of people you see yourself as per your working interest and goals in life. Always remember if you perform your job, if you are working for someone then your employer will only keep you if you are making profit for him which you can do directly yourself if you are an entrepreneur. So, always analyze this situation carefully because this will change your finances and lifestyle.

Finding the Most Joy able thing in your Work

The best things are sometimes associated with the worst which you have to go through to reach the best. The things in which you are interested, the choices you made, you should have a deep understanding of the choices you decided, from the top view its might just look like any other option of your career but, in order to find the most enjoyable thing about your work you have to break down your work in stages or look through more deeper to find what you actually like about your work, to which part of your work you are most interested or excited from which you cannot get tired of doing it every day and which is the worst part or least interested part of it which you don't like to repeat every single day. Having a sense to distinguish your interest levels in parts of your selected work will give you an advantage to measure the worthiness of going through it.

Measuring the Worth to Attain Happiness Everyday

As mentioned above at several points in your career, one has to go through hardships whether you like it or not in order to achieve the goals you have got to go through it. The difference is you will always have a choice whether you want to go through hardships or not by Measuring it's worth of happiness you attain after going through it.

In order to measure the worth of going through hardships you have to break down the work routine in different stages, in parts. So, as to analyze yourself the things which you like or interested about it or doesn't like it. once you break down in parts in the long journey the things which you have to deal within your work space and label it whether you "like it or dislike it" to each individual part of it. It will be easier for you to judge that you want to go through the hardships which you pointed out in your routine, if your hardships are lesser than the parts of which you are interested, then you can choose to find the solutions for those hardships which in turn if practice and implemented will not be considered as hardships.

When you label some part of your work hard you got to understand correctly, why are you assigning that label to that part of work, are you not interested in it or you find it genuinely difficult either way things could work out if you measure the worth of happiness you get after going through the hardships.

<u>Final Routine and Mental Readiness to adapt the minor and major changes in your life</u>

After all the steps practiced as mentioned above you will finally able to get your final routine of your work which will closely resembles the actual work routine you will get through when time comes. You will experience the major and minor changes in your work routine as you will grow and as your knowledge will increase so, you will be keep changing the things, don't be adamant of the final routine have a sense of mental readiness to change it with time and always strive to find out what actually happening in your selected field of your career, to always be ahead of your future. Always remember the changes in your final routine will have an effect on your personal development, implementation of actions will change and your requirements keep changing so, for that always have your mind open and ready to tackle anything whatever comes in your way.

CHAPTER IV

Happy Goals Realistic and Creative

Goals

Goals are very important in life, goals will give life meaning to strive every day, it will motivate every individual when the things are not going in your way, it's arouses the passion within yourself when required to face the life's hardships and unforeseen calamities. Having a goal in life will prepare you mentally, which in turn will make you ready physically. A person should be mentally strong as he will not get defeated if encounter any disastrous situations in life which are inevitable time to time, which cannot be avoided but, can go through with stronger set of mentality.

Having a Sense of Distinguishing Goals

There are different types of goals which an individual can set for themselves in different categories to mention few are personal, family goals, career related, income related respectively with the timeline. As you keep growing in your knowledge your goals will change or in your goals if there is something blank that will be filled with the increase in information. depending on what stage of life you are at present and how much information you possess will define the details of your goals along with the time line.

Categorize Realistic and Imaginative Goals

When it comes to common sense as the word speaks for itself, as having a sense which is considered to be common but, the common could be varied with your circle of knowledge to whom you relate with as your surroundings, your sources of information, will define what is common for you. To categorize your goals in realistic and imaginative you might sometime need true to be yourself, it could be a fight within yourself when it comes to categorize it as your mind and heart will not align in few of your choices and moreover, if required seek someone help of some caliber and logical individual to categorize your goals.

Getting Criticized at your Present Level

When you discuss about your plans with other individuals or they get to know about your goals they will have their own opinions. some will try to criticize badly at your face, some do back-biting, some pretend to be nice and some will motivate you it's hard to get these kind of individuals but they do exist. While, whatever everyone has to say it's based on your present level, they don't know what you are really capable off. So, never ever change your plans or goals after receiving the criticism, prove them wrong by making that happen take critics in a positive way and use it as a tool to motivate you to achieve goals for your life.

Taking Opinions of Others

Always make sure you take opinions of others never underestimate anyone's opinion as every Individual has something to offer at least the person will tell you what not to do in worst case and it will be helpful to avoid failure. this will make your mind open for the opinions, it will increase your knowledge and with every individual you will be experiencing different point of views for the same thing which will benefit your knowledge, as taking opinions doesn't mean you have to follow it this will help you in achieving different point of views for the same thing and it could only happen if different minds are giving opinions and after receiving it choose carefully to proceed with the best.

Accepting Criticism

Criticizing someone is easy but getting criticized and accepting it is hard, specially from your loved ones. slowly over the time you will develop with bear patience to accept criticism. It is important to be criticized and take that in a positive way to be motivated to reach your goals but make sure you are unaffected with the negativity around the criticism.

Settings Time Limits for Goals

Goals without the prescribed time limit are useless you have got to assign time limit for individual goal in your plan, that will boost your motivation to reach that goal within that time limit you might not hit it every time or may lose sometimes but, again time to time you have to perform altercation to your time limits as per the increment in your knowledge. The time limit which you assign to goals should be in practical limits, as your individual goal should be broken down and assigned with individual time limits to get the possible timeline as an outcome for that particular goal.

Breaking Down your Goals

In your plan you must be having a lot of goals. but, to reach that goals individually you have to breakdown individual goal with steps and further breaking down those steps if required to in order to get clarity of your goals in detail and finding about what's need to be done to achieve that goal and assigning the time limits to individual steps of your goal.

Every Goal has an Imaginative Story

Whatever goals you have in your life will have a story behind that goal or a liking towards that goal to achieve it, know your own story by analyzing your own life for every goal you must have something associated as imaginative thinking or thoughts, within the journey to achieve that goal you will think constantly about that imaginative scene when you think of your goal. Subconscious mind will have that as background in your mind when you come across something, suppose if your goal is an object a car, like an expensive car driven by you to make that subconscious part to be conscious and to use that to your advantage as your motivation will help you to achieve that goal by putting your more efforts towards that goal.

Getting a smile on your face

Happiness is everything that everyone wants in the end. But, there is always a story behind each goal that brings a smile on your face by just thinking of it now and then. you have got to identify your own happy imaginative story that will help you keep motivated through your journey and get passed through difficult times.

Determination, Distraction and Dedication

Always remember the "DDD" To achieve anything in life which stands for determination, distraction & dedication. As most of them won't give much importance to distraction that is equally important while comparing others to achieve anything in life. The most important part is identifying your distractions from which you could easily get away when you are dedicated to fulfill a task, after determining your steps of individual goals or in everyday life. Once you identify all the distractions it will be easier to provide dedication by staying away from the distractions at the time of dedication this will help you save your time in long run and help you in getting discipline. Always remember if your being lazy in identifying the distractions that will be a disaster as laziness in itself is a biggest distraction which distract individual in performing task.

Goals Missed and Achieved

In life sometimes you missed your goals or sometimes achieved. The major important part of your journey is the experience you gain while achieving the goal and if failed you should learn from your mistakes and get back on the track without repeating the mistakes, it's always to get up and never give up attitude which will lead to attain true success in life. Always strive to make yourself a better version of you.

Comparison Inspires and Destroys

Some people do compare with others and some not but while comparing with others always look towards someone below you to be thankful to God that how blessed are you and look upon someone above you for inspiration and motivation. Never let the comparison affects you personally or professionally, it will be always better to mind your own business and be focused on your goals rather comparing with others in this way your focus will be on your life not others which might ruin your life if focused on others.

CHAPTER V

Choice of Career and Effect on Life

Career Effect Imaginative on Life

Imagine how your choice for the career will impact on your life, the aspects of your imagination should include at least the basic thing that with your choice you should measure the possibility of achieving your individual goals in different categories within the timelines. It's important to be imaginative at this point to get more clarity of your future success in your life.

Career Effect Closeness to Reality

Once you have your imaginative effect of your choice on your life, compare it with the real facts by measuring it with the reality, being true to yourself or getting help from the people who are in the same field, getting their opinions on your life goals. Remember to accept the Criticism and always take positivity from the criticism as motivation to fulfill your goals.

Career Effect at Different Stages

Here you have to go in detail to assess the imaginative effect which is close to reality of your choice of the career at different stages of your life, as you did breakdown different steps for individual goals you have to do some deep analysis to that individual steps in this matter.

Career Progressive Imagination

Imagine how your career progressive graph will be like in your selected choice as it plays a vital role in measuring different levels of promotions associated with your career within the specified time limits assigned by you in your goals.

Career Progressive Graph Comparison

Once you have your imaginative career progression graph compare it with the real facts and be true to yourself or get help from the people who are in the same field take their opinions on your career progressive graph. Remember to accept the Criticism and always take positivity from the criticism as motivation to fulfill your goals.

Financial Aid to Succeed

Analyse the impact of your career decision on your present family financial situation. Some career options do require a good capital if you don't fall in that category of scholarship or if you want to go abroad for further studies it requires a separate financial planning way ahead, you should be aware of what to do in financing your career option at the right time when it comes.

Alignment of Professional and Personal Matters

Analyze the imaginative impact of your career decision effect on your future family, it depends on what point of your life you want to be settled with family by getting married and having kids. whether the timeline of your professional career is aligned with the personal preferences you have for your future family.

Career Promise

Analysis of your career in terms of progression that how much feasible or promising is your choice of the career to reach your goals within milestones. In short you have to look through on what level is your choice of your career promises. example such as easy, medium or hard to fulfill your ultimate goals within assigned timelines.

Career Pros and Cons

Be your own critique or take help from someone experienced to criticize your career journey by identifying what can possibly go wrong or what are the things which will be in your favor by looking through your career plan to reach your goals. By identifying your own pros and cons you can avoid the hurdles if avoidable or well prepared for it in advance. So, when time comes it would not be a hurdle anymore and by identifying the things which are in your favor you can take their full advantage to the possible extent.

Differentiating Forecasting, Imagination and Fortunetelling

At some point in your life when it comes to planning your future you have to be very conscious about your life, specially at the early stage of your life when majority of the students did not possess much needed clarity of their life. While planning your future an individual should be able to differentiate among forecasting, imagination and fortune telling while trying to create best possible future. While planning the future you should always go by forecasting with the strong possible basis available, a little bit of imagination if required where you cannot obtain any data is permissible but not like a fortune teller who says anything about your future without any basis or rationality.

Acceptance of Deviation from your Imagination

When you try and analyze your planning with the goals you set up along with assigned timelines in the initial stages of planning, while setting goals and timelines you will of course be imaginative of everything, at the same time be excited about your goals and achievement in your imagination, which is good but as slowly you get close to reality by analyzing your plan by time to time as per the circumstances you should not get demotivated with the deviation of your practical measurement from your imagination as it might take longer than you imagine to reach your goals. But, always remember it's not the time you are focused on but the final destination. Irrespective of how much time it will take for you to reach there you have to go for it, time after time you will be facing challenges because of the deviation from your imagination, you might feel to lose faith in your own planning but always keep the faith and confidence to proceed further in your life journey and accept the deviation as you will grow in knowledge with time.

CHAPTER VI

True to yourself

Honesty with your Own Image

Being honest in today's world, where everything seems doubtful is hard or easy depending on individual personality and his environment while growing up. For a person it's easy if its surrounding environment that includes but not limited to his friends, neighborhood and relatives are filled with honesty but, for someone whose surrounding environment lacks in honesty they may have to work hard to make a change within themself and work on to change their surrounding environment for the betterment of their own future and peace of mind.

The Biggest Cheat

After being honest with everyone you will attain peace of mind and you will progress smoothly without any burden of lies in your head. It might come as a shock to discover when you are being honest with everyone outside in your world, that you might still cheat with yourself or live in your own illusion, subconsciously about your capabilities or confident level with certain aspects of your life.

We tend to have a different image of opinions when it comes to our mind with things which are associated with us, which we don't share with anyone and we keep it with ourselves in our subconscious state of mind and sometimes we do it knowingly and being completely aware of it, at this time we are cheating ourselves that will be harmful for our future success and because of that we tend to overestimate our Capabilities or underestimate it. So, in order for us to achieve true success without wasting time, we have to fight our own complexity issues within ourselves and be true to ourselves irrespective of the consequences that will be faced. It will become much easier for your future as soon as you start being honest with you.

Distinguish between Facts and Opinions

Facts and opinions are two different things which you will come across throughout your life. So, it's better you learn to always distinguish between them and implement the same, when it comes to analyzing your career aspects and decisions of life. As you grow and learn to distinguish between facts and opinions you will find it easier to make decisions and you will have much more clarity of the situations. It is important to differentiate between them as majority of the people will be affected with other person opinion about something which is relatable and based on their opinion will take decisions and might find themselves in trouble. So, it is important to not let yourself get affected with other people's opinion.

Identifying and Verifying the Facts with Evidence

As you grow in identifying the facts while differentiating with opinions, always make sure the facts are accompanied with the true evidence and based on those facts take your decisions on your career's choice and in your life. It's time consuming process but it will be fruitful in the end, as it is mandatory specially when it comes to your major parts of your career aspects.

Being Optimistic Irrespective of Negativity

Always develop a habit of being optimistic irrespective of your negative surrounding environment, make sure you do not get affected with negativity around you and don't let your decision making skills get effected in any manner. To develop and to become optimistic you have to avoid thinking negatively about anything and talking negatively about anything and moreover, if you heard something negative your focus should be on the positive side of the story irrespective of the plot of the story to be negative.

Drawing the Line Between Confidence and Overconfidence

Drawing the line between confidence and overconfidence is important aspect of decision making skills which in turn again depends on the facts known to individual or "he think he know the facts" as an opinion in his mind. Confidence is a good thing to own it which leads to success. but, overconfidence will leads to failure or if not will lead away from the success, in both situations overconfidence will be harmful in many ways and the problem of being overconfident is sometimes you are aware of it but, still wants to go with it but, realize it later after facing the consequences of being overconfident. Confidence will be gained based on the true facts whereas, overconfidence will be gained based on the assumptions that you know the facts. So, always make sure you are confident in every situation of your life by knowing the facts related with the situation.

Ego is your Biggest Enemy

Ego as the word itself is so small but in actual it's quite big and if history is proven time after time that ego will destroy people lives and it's keep on destroying the person who has it. So, make sure you don't have it or if you possess it learn to keep it aside and do not let your ego decide your career choice or decisions. Sometimes your ego will be your biggest enemy within you that you have to fight time after time, if you need help in certain aspects of your career your ego might stop you asking help, which in turn stop your progression with that aspect. So, learn to keep aside the ego and don't let your ego get hurt on small matters of day to day life, in the end always remember it's you who decide how to react when life becomes tough.

Listing Facts about Career Choice

Always get your facts right and know the facts about your choice of the career which provides you a bigger clarity to achieve success in future and mold your personality as per the requirements of your career choice. List out all the facts available about the choice of your career and goals as much as possible for every stage of your career.

Information on your Career Choice

Get information or opinions as and when required accordingly for the choice of your career or goals from the people which are in the same field. Sometimes you might not get insightful or important information about any niche career from other sources then from the real people who has experience in that same field you are chosen, which in turn could be very helpful and informative to attain success.

Opinions From Achievers and Failures

Take opinions from everyone you know from the same field which you chose from the achievers and failures. Take note of everything they have to offer if possible to differentiate the pros and cons of the opinions and analyze the facts from the opinions.

Avoiding the Facts that Lead to Failures

After getting the opinions from others, list out all the facts you came across which leads to failure and keep a regular check on it. So, that you are not committing the same mistakes in order to avoid failure and get close to success.

Introvert, Extrovert and Intelligent

There are advantages and disadvantages of being an introvert and extrovert that depends on individual level of intelligence. As introvert keep things to himself, if he is intelligent enough will figure out other ways to get information without taking other opinions. where, as an extrovert will have an advantage of taking opinions from others and with the level of intelligence both can decide their career. An introvert will lack an option of interaction with others and will be limited to options which are in his comfort level.

Categorizing the Information

After getting the information from all the sources you categorize the information belongs to "facts or opinions" you may find it much easier if you follow it for better understanding and clarity of taking decisions for your career. When you do categorize it do it with utmost honesty without being biased towards the things which you feel are in your favor.

Conscious Decisions

Throughout the journey of your planning and after planned stage as well, while updating your goals, timelines and activities in your career graph, you have to be very conscious while performing it, always be active. Do not take any decisions subconsciously specially the important ones, make sure you find a way to be active, avoid the time when you are tired when planning important parts of your career graph.

CHAPTER VII

Personality Development

Definition of Personality Development in Simple Terms

The process of adding skills to your personality or Enhancing the skills you already possess or updating it with time along with the growth around you is personality development.

Difference between Developed and Development

Difference between developed and development in simple term is developed is where the object is already developed there is no further requirement of enhancement while, development is the process of continued improvement or Enhancement.

Identify the Required Development

It's important that you identify in which of the areas you are required development to achieve your goals in respective categories such as, physical goals, personal goals, academic goals & professional goals. You have to identify your present level of skills in each and every aspect that will impact on your goals and career, to be prepared it in advance, plan about their respective solutions, implement it in your planning effectively and monitor your progress regularly. With this you will reduce the chances of failure and increase your chances to become successful.

Identifying your Own Drawbacks

Drawbacks are setbacks if not conquered at the right time, with the right approach to overcome it. Initially with complete honesty you have to identify your own drawbacks, within this part you got to be true to yourself after identifying it. find the appropriate solutions to overcome it, as it will avoid the failures and remove your own hurdles to get closer towards success.

Opinions on Drawbacks

It is no harm in taking opinions of others to find your own drawbacks with an open mind by welcoming criticism. It is important for you to take opinions from others in this matter as sometimes, we do miss out on our own drawbacks and others opinions could be very helpful to identify it. Make sure you do take opinions on your academics, physical, personal & professional drawbacks respectively with the respective individuals and then analyze their opinions before passing any kind of judgment and incorporate respective solutions for your drawbacks in your planning to overcome it.

Categorization of Drawbacks

When you do take opinions from others make sure you categorize your drawbacks based on academics, physical, personal and professional categories. You got to remember to be always keep your mind open and welcome criticism in this categories as mostly the persons which are close to you will be able to provide their opinions, as the opinions which are related with your personal drawbacks your colleagues and friends could provide their opinions, for your academics your professors and lecturers will be helpful not just the opinions on your drawback but, they could even suggest you for the solution, for your physical drawbacks you can able to figure it out if your career option requires physical fitness as mandatory requirement and for your professional drawbacks, that will be hypothetical based on your present level.

Overcome your Drawbacks

while you work out to overcome your own drawbacks make your approach realistic as what's needed to be done to overcome your drawbacks with a honest and realistic approach. If require take someone's help to overcome your drawbacks.

Monitor your Progress

Monitor your progress towards your personality development and own drawbacks by measuring it with the respective activity related to the developments and drawbacks. If the activity cannot be measured with the numbers break it down in steps and then measure it but, find a way to measure the progress, if not you might lose interest which might be very harmful for your career, as anything which you feel is need to be developed or overcome in case of drawback, will play vital role in your career graph to underestimate any activity in this matter will be foolishness specially, after knowing the activities and their respective solutions.

Assigning the Timeline

After listing out all the personality developments need to be done and drawbacks to overcome within yourself in different categories, assign the timelines to individual activity with respective goals in a realistic approach, to monitor and measure your own progress in a timely manner.

Hobbies to Develop your Personality

Personality development could be easier if you find a hobby which eventually helpful to develop your skills in the respective category to which the hobby is relatable. You have to identify hobbies for all the possible categorize of personality development and for the drawbacks which requires to overcome, as it will be helpful and gives more chances for you to be focused on the development while having fun doing it.

Personality Development for Life

Personality development is a phenomenon which you have to adapt throughout your life in order to maintain success in your life. You always have to keep yourself updated with the surroundings and environmental changes, as you grow in knowledge you will identify how beneficial it is for your career progress. The personality development will help in reaching new heights of success in your career graph.

Extrovert edge over Introvert

As discussed in the preceding chapter the advantages of being an extrovert by welcoming criticism, if needed this could also be developed by practicing in everyday life as, making a habit to talk with one stranger a day or whatever suits you to overcome from being introvert as it will gives you a lot of advantage being an extrovert specially, for the parts mentioned in this chapter which required having opinions from others.

CHAPTER VIII

Requirements to Achieve Goals

Preparation of Identifying the Requirements

Preparation in itself is self-examine that's need to be done with full consciousness and caution throughout your career journey and throughout your life. Everything you wanted to do in your life needs a preparation, that is the initial stage of something to be achieved in time and if your preparations are strong, then your results will be excellent. So, identifying the requirements to achieve your goals is a big task, as you have to identify the futuristic requirements for some aspects of your career, which sometimes could not be easy.

Assessment of Requirements

Once you listed out all the requirements for all the goals that you have planned during this stage, as it requires a lot of planning and a lot of information need to be processed. After that you must have got the individual requirements for your individual broken down activity respectively for individual goals. While you go through this preparation stage you may find yourself in exhaustive stage, with all the information and sometimes you may assign the requirements incorrectly or missed something or assign additional requirement to your activity, in order to avoid all these things it is better if you assess all the requirements with respective goals and activity once before finalizing it. So, you don't have any error in your requirements to achieve the goals.

Improvising Level of Requirements

The requirements which you can identify today might not remain the same until the time you start your professional career. As it could happen a lot of things which are associated with your career graph might keep changing over the time. So, always make sure you are updated with the time by improvising the level of requirements when needed. So, you are always ready to go one step closer towards success.

Importance of Commitment

Commitment is very important aspect of being successful and it plays major role in defining success and in your case you have to be committed to the choice of your career, the goals you have chosen, along with the steps which you have elaborated for individual goals. without being committed towards those goals and career choice which you made for yourself it is impossible to attain success.

Importance of Integrity

Integrity is the best quality a human being can possess, which makes him a great gentleman with strong definitive high moral values and complete honesty which leads to satisfaction of your soul, irrespective of the results whether it is failure or success. A person with integrity always follow the path of honest man with high moral values for him the goals and career are equally important when compared to a person who if, require sacrifice honesty to gain something out of it. Majority of them in today's world will look for the options which are not genuine to achieve their goals but a honest man will not sacrifice his honesty instead he will be happy to leave the goal behind which ask him to compromised his honesty, as success for him not lies in just achieving the goals but, achieving the goals keeping his honesty, self-respect and moral values.

Importance of Determination

Determination the word itself teaches us without determination nothing is possible, as you have to possess the firmness of determination on your chosen path to explore your successful journey with stronger determined attitude towards your goals. Determination is something if you have to practice on daily basis as per your daily goals if, you are not determined to do what's need to be done then you are surely determining the failure. Determination is one of the aspect that will leads to success. The stronger your determination for your goals and career the bigger your success will be in future.

Importance of Focus

Focus is the most important aspect of your success throughout your life without being focused you cannot do anything in life, your focus should be on everything which gets you closer towards success. if you lose your focus it will cost you dearly in terms of delays with your goals and assigned timelines. To attain true success you always got to be focused.

Importance of Positive Energy

Importance of being positive all the time, by thinking positive always keep your mind positive, as it will benefits in the end. With all the circumstances you face, all the hurdles you come across, you should think that all these difficulties you will come across will makes you stronger than before and without facing difficulties, hardships no one has got real success and after facing difficulties, hardships if you got success. This success will be a greater success as it will rewards you for your difficulties and hardships you faced throughout your journey.

Identifying Biggest Distraction

Everyone will have distractions specially, when they are focused on to do something, that's very normal. You have to identify your distractions and list them out to point out your biggest distraction, as it will be very helpful for you to attain success, as distractions will consume a lot of your precious time. So, learn to identify your distractions time to time, as it will vary with time and growth. learn to avoid them to get closer to success.

Ways to Overcome Distraction

Find simple ways to overcome distractions, the best way is to stick to your daily routine and avoid the distractions by following your routine with complete honesty without being lazy, always think of your goals which eventually drives you towards motivation to put your efforts every day.

The Most Valuable Thing in Life "Time"

Time is the most valuable asset you possess which cannot be replaced with anything in the world. So, make sure you do identify it's preciousness, if you incur loss of money it can be recovered with time but, once you lose time it cannot be recovered. When you think of your time consider it as your most valuable currency, which you have to spend every day. so, you do make in advance planning where and with whom you want to spend time in near or far future.

Time Management by Categories

If you can manage time you can manage anything, being said that the first thing if you want to do any work you have to learn the time management. So, by categorizing your activities and assigning the time to it on daily basis will help you in time management

Moreover, have your priorities set along with the difficulties level of activities, the most difficult one's should goes first as it gives you a satisfaction on completion of it and helps in providing you motivation to complete the rest of the activities. So, that when you go to sleep you will be satisfied for the day and be ready for your next day.

Practice Time Management

Follow your routine along with the time management like a robot, don't think of yourself as human being when it's comes to follow your routine, as human tends to show laziness which will not be good, the least you can do is follow your daily routine 90 percent of the time on monthly basis, try to cover that missing part on weekends. Think as if you are instructing yourself to follow your routine irrespective of tiredness, unwillingness or laziness. Always remember the reason you take not to perform task will be just an excuse, that will take you away from success and closure to failure. So, you better decide where you want to be end up and whom you want to become in future. Your daily actions and routine will define your level of success you will attain in future.

CHAPTER IX

Winner or Loser by Choice

<u>Understanding a winner</u>

A winner is someone who wins all the time or majority of the time by putting his efforts every day, by polishing his skill which is the underlying asset for him to be a winner. A winner has, never give up attitude, he always strive to become a better version of him, he doesn't compare or compete with anyone but with him, in sports you will see winners after he wins with the opponent but, in his mind he has to give his best no slightest of compromise is allowed if you want to become a winner.

<u>Understanding a Successful Person</u>

Being Successful person in itself is a unstoppable journey, until you decided to stop or the circumstances will lead you or flipped you away from success. Understanding, if you want to become a successful person just by achieving some goals in your initial stage of life or carry on doing it for the rest of your life. Success is based on your satisfaction with your goals or career. If you are truly happy and satisfied with the level of success in your life then you slowdown in terms of achievements, your greediness will be less when compared to your previous version. Not many people will stop but, go further as they wants to attain new heights of success by achieving new goals, at last your happiness and peace of mind will define your success, with the inner utmost satisfaction you attain after all the hardships you go through in your successful journey.

Own Definition of Success

Definition of Success varies with every individual irrespective of the same goals, as the success is purely based on the journey you take from the beginning, all the hardships, obstacles and people you overcome in your journey while protecting your honesty and moral values throughout your journey. The dedication you put in for your commitment towards your goals, with the determination you work on by keeping your focus, keeping the positive energy while overcoming the criticism will define your success. In the end your true happiness with utmost satisfaction will make you a successful person.

Understanding a Loser

A loser is someone who failed to meet a criteria which Society defines or he himself in his life defines for his career. A loser will be a loser up until he wins in his life attain success. but, if a loser at that point of time give up don't proceed to come back or find an alternative completely different thing in which he failed again don't come back, then he will be considered as a loser and he keeps repeating that with everything he does in his career then he is really a loser.

People think loser becomes just like that but every loser has his own story they must have worked hard or not or did not worked hard enough to meet the criteria to achieve the goals. Sometimes in life we become overconfident or lack of motivation tends to keep us away from success and the consequences will be of a loser. Not many people understand by not doing anything in life you are everyday getting close of becoming a loser. It's never late to start your planning to do something in your life to become successful.

Understanding a Failure

Failure is a part of successful journey as majority of them failed at first. but, as they learn from their reasons of failure, they will get improve every time they failed by avoiding or not repeating the same thing which lead them to failure. Failure will teach you a lot if you wanted to learn from it and you will become a better version of you once you start embracing failure and starts learning from it.

Differentiating Between a Loser and a Winner

The biggest difference between a loser and a winner is simple but yet you have to understand it and always remember it that a loser once loose will give up on it and never come back and will find excuses to not come back and will blame other individuals or other things for his failure. Whereas a winner always strives to come back and learn from his failures, embrace the failure with full responsibility on him and will always keep right attitude to never give up.

Understanding There is Always a Choice

There is always a choice associated with everything in life, you have to understand the importance of its association with everything you come across in your life and throughout your career. You will become eventually the product of your choices. So, make sure you know the values of your decisions, there will be always a choice to do a thing or not to do it.

Understanding Regrets

Majority of the people will have regrets in their life, some admit and accept it some won't. Regrets are made of your own choices, you have to understand it, if you are regretting something then you shouldn't repeat it and learn from it, understand it is the past you cannot do anything about it, if you keep your regrets in your mind they will definitely spoil your present and future. Sometimes, we do regret about something in future but when we took that decision back in time, that was exactly what you wanted to do because of the situation. So, there shouldn't be actually any regrets always keep your focus on your future every day is a new day you are alive that is the biggest blessing.

Identifying your Positive Habits

Identify your positive habits by careful analysis, it will help you in one way or the other, if you know your positive habits you can take advantage of it when it comes to your career and goals. By acknowledging your positivity you can utilize it when required. So, it's always better to know yourself and be aware of your habits.

Identifying your Negative Habits

Identify your negative habits if any, by careful analysis don't be biased while performing it, the more honest you are while doing it, the more helpful it will be for your future. After knowing your negative habits try to avoid it as it will one way or other will destroy your future. Your negative habits will go against your future if not rectified immediately.

Effects of Positive and Negative Habits

Analysis of your positive and negative habits effect on your career progression and your goals. Habits consume time so, you know time is the prime factor as where we have to spend it and with whom and if it's related with your health it might have major impacts on your future.

Overcoming your Negative Habits

There is always a way to overcome anything in life you just have to find a way to overcome your negative habits if any, with complete honesty by putting your efforts as in the beginning everything looks difficult but, as you go through this difficult times you will adapt living without your negative habits and as time progress you will be happy about it and it will leave a positive impact on your life and provides you with self confidence that you can do anything in life.

Clarity of Life

Clarity of life is a very important factor to live your life to the fullest, with the utmost satisfaction and to know the clarity of your life, your choices you make should be clearly based on rational thinking. Having clarity of life needs planning in advance with well defining goals and rational thinking about your career options. If you don't have clarity of life, it will be like someone who took a journey without assigning a destination. Just imagine that you started your car and took a driving seat and you don't know which way to go then how you will feel about it. So, in order to have clarity of life everything should be planned.

CHAPTER X

Comparison

Career Comparison

Check the Choice of your career based on your grades and interests are same or if different Compare them in detail by giving each of the option a priority over the other.

Comparing the Basis

Comparison of basis of selection of your choice by grades and interest, which leads to your career's choice respectively and comparing the influencing criteria to reach for those choices by grades and interest respectively.

Career Practicality Level

Comparing your imaginative level progression with the practical statistics to know the clarity and depth of your career progression.

Deciding Factors

Listing out all the factors of your career choice as per the grades and interest. Analyze the deciding factor in both cases to finalize it.

Prioritizing the factors and its effect on life

Assigning priority to all the listed factors and its effect on your life.

Final Choice

Final choice of your career based on the priority assigned to the factors associated.

CHAPTER XI

Nature of Success and Failure

Nature of Success

Every individual has to keep in his conscious mind, the nature of success is temporary, it should not affect your confidence level to become overconfident which will be harmful in maintaining success.

Nature of Failure

Failure is temporary don't make the failure turns out for you to become a loser.

Maintaining Success

After attaining success it's important to stick to basics which leads to success to keep it maintained.

Avoiding Failures

With lack of planning you get close to failure, with everything planned in detailed failures can be avoided to some extent of the factors which are controllable.

Acceptance of Failure

Acceptance of failure is an important skill need to be learned with time and open mind, as it is one of the most important part of success is how you deal with your failures and how fast you overcome your failures to start next chapter of your life without thinking of your failure but, learning from it and not repeating the things which leads to failure.

Identifying Depression

When you go through tough times you might find yourself in depression subconsciously but, you will not be aware of it. You have to identify that stage in your life if you are going through depression, as it could be very harmful to continue in that state for your health and career.

Fighting Depression

You have got to find a way to fight depression and overcome it with the positivity around you by counting your blessings, the positive things happening in your life. Depression it's the early stage where your mind will give up before your body, physically it's very hard to get noticed by someone if you are going through it, unless you are very much in depression and failed to identify it early.

Always Remember Temporary State

Everything in this world is temporary, always remember that no matter what happens time will pass through it and time will heal every pain, you just have to stay positive in difficult times, that can only be possible if you keep practicing to stay positive all the time and make that as a habit.

Reality of Life

The bitter truth of life is death, one day everyone has to die that's inevitable for everyone, no one can escape death when time comes you will leave this world, always keep this in mind as then only you won't get affected by the failures you have to go through in your life.

Adapting Healthy Lifestyle

Healthy lifestyle adaption is the key to success. By exercising, eating healthy food and getting enough sleep. Your body is a weapon and life is not less than a war so, in order to win the war your weapon should be strong with all the aspects required to win the war. Never compromise on healthy lifestyle as it might affect your other routines which are related with your career and personal life.

Practicing Honesty for Peace of Mind

The most important thing is peace of mind to live longer and healthier in order to attain that, practice honesty in everything you deal, irrespective of the consequences this will make you stay humble and will gain trust, respect in the society and the most important part is you will have your dignity.

Avoiding Fakeness

Avoid being fake or getting validation from others for your decisions. Always be yourself don't think of what others will think or say if you do something. unless your action might hurt someone's feelings and if they do so then proceed with utmost polite manner.

Prepare to Face High and Low of Life

Mentally be prepare to face high and low of life, always be ready for the unexpected situations to come in your life and remember you can't control the unexpected situations but, what you can control is how you will react towards it, by giving your best eventually you will come out more stronger.

Conclusion

Every individual gets the same time 24 hours every day, the difference is your own choice that you make every day for your career and personal life. In the end always remember you will be the product of your own choices. So, take it very carefully and embrace it gracefully and follow it obediently to attain success in life.

ABOUT THE AUTHOR

Mohammed Mustafa Ali

My work experience I had worked as Project Coordinator in Kuwait in a Korean company before that I did work as a sales representative in London. I have Master's Degree in Petroleum Technology from Teesside University and Bachelor's Degree in Chemical Technology despite having those degrees I had very little experience working as a heavy oil engineer at Weatherford international and that made me write this book.